SCENES FROM
A FIRE ESCAPE
BY DANIEL STETZEL

I0081259

UNDERWATER MOUNTAINS PUBLISHING
LOS ANGELES, CALIFORNIA
A SECRET COMPANY.

SCENES FROM A FIRE ESCAPE BY DANIEL STETZEL

EDITED AND ARRANGED BY DUNIGAN GAFFORD
COVER ART BY MICKEY HARMON

This book is dedicated to My Family. Mom, Dad, Lauren, Mat, and my dogs, Lexi and King Japhy, thank You for always believing in Me, even when I was losing faith in Myself. Without Your love and support, I'd be a goner by now. The Stetzels, Hagbergs, Wilburs, Suraces, Andersons, I love y'all. To Uncle Cliff who told me long ago I had "IT!" My friends Joe, Justin, Greg, D-Rock, Warren Boogie, and Mickey, for being there to support me when I needed a kind hand to get Me back on track. This is for Fitz, Jordan, and Matt at the Pink who are always ready with a shot of whiskey, a beer, and a friendly smile. This is for all the Women I've loved, and hated, for inspiring Me to write a lot of these silly poems. Lastly, this is for My dear friend and neighbor Molly, for putting up with my shit over the last few years, I truly appreciate you, but FFS. &Eli

Without all of you in my life, these words would surely not exist, thank you.

...Mama, I did it!

Scenes from a
Fire Escape

by
Daniel
Stetzel

Feet Dangling, Spitting on Passersby

Sometimes,
standing outside
of the bar,
slowly enjoying
inhalations of
death,
I catch bits of
vapid conversation,
and I find Myself
wanting to grab hold
of them and yell;

"This is not the time
for senseless inanity,
Now is the time
for senseless
living!"

We were both kids
with fucked up upbringings,

Both of Our parents
hated each other,

though neither pair divorced
because They were Roman Catholic,

We smoked a lot of pot
and cigarettes,

We drank liquor We stole
from Our parents' cabinets,

We stole shit and
fingered girls in dugouts
behinds High Schools
in the suburbs
at midnight,

He developed a habit for H.
I for words,

He kicked His and had a kid,
I didn't and own a dog
and somehow We're still alive,

through it all,

though neither of Us
could've ever said
We'd be here now
when We were 13.

I was born
and then I grew,
and They threw
the pieces at Me
and told me,
Now build!

Now build!

Build something new.
out of nothing,
but don't let it
teeter, tremble. or topple,
if it falls that's the
death of only you,

We'll be fine,
We gave You the pieces,

Now build,
build something new,
if You start now
you might finish
before you're dead;

I looked at the pieces.

We passed
a joint, getting
high on the
edge of the roof
of an old warehouse
building looking
over the East side
of the City,

the lights of
downtown sparkled
in the distance
like a beacon
calling us forth,

but we dangled
our legs over
the asphalt abyss
below, talking in
feverish circles
like mad prophets
of long ago,

and in this
moment void of time
We became
endless.

Spare Me your
convoluted and
overly contrived
notions about
suffering,

Eat tuna
out of the
can for a
week straight,

and stress over
whether or not
You can pay rent
on time this month,

or afford to buy
a pack of smokes
after the gas bill
was paid,

then tell Me
what it's like
to suffer
just a little.

It meant something
It meant everything
It meant nothing,

It lost its meaning
   along the way,

It became a question
   of meaningful
         meaninglessness,

   along the way,

It was fluorescent shards,
It was the local bar bully,
It was a shot to the Manhood,
It was
It was
It was

            exactly what
                  its was,

Fuck it,

We burn the city down
            and rebuild,

   from the ground up.

I stood firm.
the tempest
could not shake
Me!

The hail fell
like biting
wasps,

but I would not
be deterred!

I clenched my
teeth &

balled My fists,

I was prepared,

to crush everything
in my path,

                                for War,

the storm sensed this,
and
trembled
in
Fear,

and rightfully
so.

I have had
black eyes,
bloody noses,
split lips,

I know what it's like
to bleed
a little,

My ribs & pride
have been bruised
on more than one occasion,

We fought with
a furious
nature,

Our Fathers worked
in factories,
cut raw meat,
drove pick-ups,

We were born
with a
furious nature,

Our quarrels weren't those
of meaningless rows
between boys,

rather a preparation
for the lives
We would lead;

Warriors.

I sat on the
Fire Escape
a little after
Sunrise on a
Sunday, watching
a woman walking
a tiny dog
down the sidewalk,
the dog was wearing
an equally tiny sweater,
and the thought struck Me;

It's someone's job
to sit at a machine
all day sewing
tiny fucking sweaters
for dogs.

I took a sip
of My coffee,

I sit at a machine
all night creating
whatever the fuck
I want,

I guess I don't
have it that bad
after all.

You're not as
vivid as so-and-so,

You lack the imagery,
and detail compared to
    what's-his-name,

Why do You always
write about booze and Women?

I would rather read
_____, they're much
    more romantic;

I rebut;

So go read their shit,
and stay the fuck out
        of My tomb.

I never wanted to be
    one of Them;

the beautiful crowd;

I never would be
I knew what knuckles
on bone felt like,

I knew what it was
like having to drag
Myself off the dirt
after being knocked down,

I wanted to be notorious,
I wanted them to look
away in fear of My
vicious snarl,

I never wanted to fit in,
I wanted to stand out,
I wanted Them to loathe Me,

because I knew if They did,

They would never be able
    to beat Me.

I was consistently angry,

standing in line for coffee,
sitting still in traffic,
waiting in the doctor's office,

I punched holes in
             walls
             doors
street signs,
    buildings,

I became the embodiment
         of pure destruction,

I began to believe scars
    were points of strength,

and the blood letting from
    my knuckles was pain
     "leaving the body,"

What an ignorant fool
         I was,

but anger will do that
         to a Man.

I am plunging
into the flames
head first,

(Is there any other
way?)

The outcome is
never guaranteed,

(Life?)

More of Us will
make it
after we rot,

Than We will while
living,

(Posthumous)

The burn is only
temporary,

(the victory is
Immortality.)

What did I care
what They expected?

    I've got thick skin
and I can start a fire
    with a flint and
        some steel,

    I'll survive,

And why did I even want
    to fit into their way
        of being?

    the preposterous
    nature of it all
        was sickening,

    But I knew Their
        tricks so
    My perspective
        never faltered,

I'd finger-paint
La scaux walls &
die unknown before

        folding to the
        status quo.

I
dread
the day
I become
a beast
of
prediction

when
the
patterns of
a
wild animal
are
discovered
it is
as good as
dead.

We begged when We
     needed to,
and stole what We
     couldn't afford,

We were promised the
Sun, Moon, & Stars,

But were awarded only
     bruised ribs &
     bloody noses,

Our parents weren't
     rich or proud,

and We took Our beatings
     with gritted teeth,

So yeah,
         We begged
         We stole
         We suffered,

   with no remorse,
     or regret,

and We never looked back.

I knocked the dirt
        off my boots &
stepped through the doorway
        of memory,

MOTHER! FATHER!

It is I!

Your Son!

Am I the visitant
You envisioned?

MOTHER! FATHER!

Your arms can defend
Me no longer!

How I yearn for Your
gentle hands
that
safeguarded Me for
so many years!

How I grovel for Your amnesty!

How I desire the
liberation of
childhood!

MOTHER! FATHER!

am I what You expected
    to walk trough Your door?

Undergo a singular
        path,

Do not accept the consolation
        of walking
            upon
        the back
            of
        Another,

the words &
        actions &
        lessons of
                others
will only teach You
                so much,

        Build
        Your Own
Goddamn
        bridge.

To those that broke My heart,
To those that broke My bones,
To those that broke My faith;

You never really broke anything,
You only forced Me to recognize
My weaknesses, and grow stronger
because of them

You Fools don't realize,
You were only throwing gasoline

On My flames.

The Con Man,
The Holy Con Man,

That Lover of

               eccentric
               sophisticated

     Women,

That indifferent Desperado
sitting in the train station
sipping on a cigarette
with an assured grace:

How envious I was of those
unperturbed outcasts &
rebels against expectancy;

I wanted to be
               Lucas Jackson,
               Jim Stark,
               Josey Wales;

but the courage wasn't in Me,
       just yet,

and so I settled for experiencing
   the life of a deviant,
             an outlaw,
           a rebel,

   through vicarious eyes.

     for now.

The menu was
extremely limited;

mostly consisting of
pasta & tuna fish outta
the can, because it was
cheap & easy & it kept
        Me fed,

I always kept low-shelf
beer in the fridge for
            when I needed
        to be drunk,

I stretched a pack of
    smokes as long as
        I could, or resorted
    to rolling My own
            from leftover
                butts,

But Me & the dog
slept well, &
grew lean & dangerous,
we were sharp
& consistently
aware, We were only
making due in reality,

But in Our reality,
making due was enough
to keep Us hungry.

We were vicious
          creatures
looking for a fight,

          fist on bone on
                    crushed veneer,

spitting blood,
spitting mad,

          ; My Brother's guttural noise ;

"one more word, and I'll
 fucking kill You,"

          ; Fear living in His eyes ;

People learn to keep Their
          distance,

     around
                    vicious creatures.

They show Me
pictures of their
pets,
and kids
and fiancés,

and they're so
fucking happy
and I just Am,

it makes me laugh,

because I know I
could beat the shit
outta them all,

They fight for
what they have
to live for,

but I fight
because I'm not
afraid to die
for anything.

Grow a
hard
gut,

learn to
stomach
the
turmoil,

grow a
hard
chin,

learn to
take
a
punch,

Men
with
weak guts
and
weak chins
never
become
World-Shakers.

There is nothing
left for Me here,

I have not planted
any roots in soil,

merely secured the
anchor against the
tear of the current,

There is nothing
left for Me here,

I will flee this City,

like clouds fleeing
from the black sky,

until Life is
empty and beautiful,

and I am alone with
        my thoughts.

There are sinners
        on the back
                porch.

Smoking cigarettes,

     While Saints knock on
              the front
                 door,

Selling Redemption,

         She's wearing
            hand-me-
           downs,

And I can barely
    afford rent,

Our different realities
     are all similarly

        torturous.

I was raised a Roman
catholic, but I only prayed
on nights when I
thought I was dying;

"Dear God! Dear Jesus! Dear Madonna!"

I would plead,

"I'm dying! I think I'm
dying! I'm afraid of
dying! Please don't
let Me Die!"

I promised;

> Church on Sundays,
> Abstain from Sex,
> Prayers at Meals,
> No Blasphemies,
> Strict devotions,
> & piousness,

Then I'd fall asleep
and wake up the next
morning & shed My
promises,

I would forget
> God, Jesus, Holy Madonna,

> Until the next time I
> thought I would Die;

Because that's how I thought
the game went.

Emotionally bankrupt,
burnt out,
Vices,

Sedative & Soliloquies,
and
last nights leftovers,

A closet full of aluminum,
A chest full of Tin,

Crafted of Chaos,

The perfected art of
Seduction,

Compiled on the
laundry list
of
Melancholy.

Crushed by the weight
of an
allegory,

brain wracked
by the
consequences
of tomorrow,

standing in the
eye
of the
storm

can be calming,

if You're
at peace

with the
inevitable.

allow Yourself
to be
at
Peace.

Suppose I told You
everything You ever thought to
be true was a falsity?

That Love was merely a
chemical reaction in Your brain,
That the sky wasn't
really blue, just bad reflections,
That the Sun never
really rises or sets, mere illusions,
That there is no God,
simply a safety net constructed
because of a fear of
the unknown;

Could You, Should You, Would You,
believe in My truths,

or can You devise
Your own?

Take Your time,

This is Important.

Sneaking Down the Ladder at the Blossoming Sun

The jig was up,
Our Love was shot
and We both knew it,

Still We scrambled
to put it back together
but it slipped through
Our fingers like
sand castles into the Sea,

We had nothing but
good intentions but
the flame had long since
burned out, and
We neglected to stoke
the fire out of
apathy and disregard
for the cold,

So We salvaged what
was left of Ourselves
and went Our separate ways,

I knew She would
fall into the arms of Love
again sometime soon,
probably with a better Man
than I,

and the thought of
sleeping alone
was comforting
for a change.

We drove on the
same highways, roads,
    streets,

the same places,
different universes,

      I was years ahead,
      She years behind,

      I wasn't what
      She needed,

      She wasn't what
      I wanted,

      Rifts in time &
      Sweet lullabies,

      Are We Paradigms?

Are We the pieces of
the puzzle that end up
swept under the rug?

I shaved
once before
a writing class
I was taking
after growing
an untamed beard
that made Me look
like a wild-person,

I walked in the room
and the girls immediately
took notice,
Some of them winked,
some motioned as if to say,
"You look great!"

They smiled big
and made eyes,

it was funny how
They took notice,

and I took notice of
Them noticing Me,

and I couldn't have
cared less –

it only went to show
that They were
only interested in
the surface of
My story.

Forever ago,

We were really something,

Young & Beautiful & Unafraid,

We adventured into countless night,
hand in hand, backs to the setting Sun,
Our apocalypse was the darkness,
We were unstoppable together,
2 beautiful silhouettes,

3 great years, and then came
the end, followed by the depression,

5 years went by like a single night's sleep,

and there You were, standing in the
produce aisle, shopping for lettuce,

We exchanged formalities,
How are You's,
What have you been up to's,
and then parted,
You towards the frozen foods,
Me towards Dairy,

and it seems like Forever Ago,

but God,

We were really something.

"Your sorry isn't
 worth shit!"

I knew that,

"You're a real
 piece of work,
 did Ya know that?"

I knew that.

"I would've been
 good to You,
 ya fucking idiot,"

I knew that,

"You're going to
 end up alone, just
 You and Your dog,"

I knew that,

"And just so You know,
 Your poetry is
 pretty fucking awful,"

I knew that.

If You
were here now
We would walk
hand in hand
down these
frozen avenues,

kept warm
by the fact
that We were
trudging through
this Hell
together.

I needed Your
voice to believe
in the future,

I found Myself
jealous of the
roof of Your mouth
where Your
tongue touched,

To taste Your
lips would be
to experience
an endless
possibility.

Quid quo pro, Jack;

You ever meet the Devil?

I have,
She wore a soft bra
and red panties,
passed out
on the futon,

only I didn't
know it until
just now,

it struck Me
like a bullet
through the brain.

I am not the
Love I consistently
write about.

Maybe I was
at one point
a while back,
when I was
younger.

Now,
I'm exhausted by
the whole silly
business of it all.

I don't make
time for it, nor
do I trust it much
anymore.

But I get that
familiar feeling,
now and then,
when I roll out of
their beds in
the morning and yawn,
forgetting
where I am,
and how I
got there.

We drank and smoked
cigarettes until the
sun came out from
behind the moon's shade,
then, laying in bed
We mashed wet lips
until I though mine
were going to bust open,
Our hands searched
warm and smooth flesh
pressed together under
the tangle of sheets
until We fell asleep
tangled in limbs,
in the afternoon we
woke and drank coffee
on the porch in the
wake of tremulous
hangover felicity,
She drove Me back
to My place, and before
I opened the door to
get out of Her car
She looked at Me with
gravely earnest eyes
and said;

"If You don't want to
   see me again it's fine...
   I'll just pretend
   you died."

She asked me how the
frigid North East was,

I told Her - cold, and
very unforgiving,

It's lonely, I said,
All We want is something
warm waiting for Us
at the end of the day,

Come to L.A. She told Me,

I would Love to, if I had
the money and courage to
leave the security of
my secure isolation,

and if I did, I don't
know if I'd ever come back,

but maybe that wouldn't
                    be a bad thing.

Only a fool
who sleeps
alone,

makes the bed
in the morning,

Only fools
trust a compass,

instead of instinct,

When My gut tells
Me "Flee!"

I leave wakes of dust,

When my gut screams
"Stand still!"

I build monuments,

I have grown to trust
my gut,

and I never make the bed
in the morning.

A victim of the perils
of certain fate,

Contaminated by Your
vulgar bliss,

But You perverted Love
by speaking so frequently
about it,

I grew immune to Your disease,
shedding You like last years skin,

I would flourish alone
or die in the process,

but I would not stand to
let You torture My bones

any longer.

I've never needed
   anyone before,

and if You don't
   want Me,

then, Sweetheart,
I don't need You,

I have made it this far
   on My own,

I will admit that it
   won't be easy,

but when has Life
ever been easy?

There I was,
cheek
to cheek,
trying to seduce
this blue-eyed
Devil,

We slow danced
on sagging streets,
under the
Harvest moon,

And in the morning
while she slept,
I crept away
towards the a blossoming Sun,

My soul still intact.

I wanted to say hello,
I wanted to talk to

                     You,

but I'm really only

                    Good

when I'm hiding behind
     My typewriter,

I hope You won't hold
     it against Me,

I saw You, Maybe looking
     at me
   (I could only hope)

Perhaps Tomorrow
will be different?

   Goodnight,
 (Or morning)

    Hi.

We fucked and
screamed and
fought, viciously,

We went for each other's
throats with such intensity
that the universe should
have come unraveled,

but it never did,

and in the morning,
when We awoke,
Our eyes preached forgiveness,

and We did the best We could,
to rebuild the structure
We had broken;

Our Love was the
tearing down,
and,
rebuilding,
of Our structure.

She would wake up
early most days and
    dress quickly, then
    leave with a quick
peck and goodbye,

    Sometimes She would
stay for coffee, but
    We never really talked
    much on those occasions,

    She would climb into
bed, pressing Her large
    soft breasts against
my chest as My hands
    traced her curving
    hips down Her thighs,

    and when We fucked
there was nothing behind
    Her eyes, nothing that
    extended into any sort
    of emotional territory,
        for Her it was just
warm skin on skin and
        wet lips, and I learned
        to take it for what
        it was, and nothing more,

        and when She finally
        left Me for good,
        I didn't feel like I
            lost much.

They laughed together,
jumping like maniacs,

I sat on the edge of
the roof overlooking
silent streets,
parking lots,
sleeping homes,

He made Her laugh
like I never could,

They had something
I never would,

They were young
and free and
careless,
attacking life
with reckless
abandonment,

He made Her laugh
like I never could
like I never would,

while I sat on the edge
watching,

      like I always did.

She asked;

> "When did You believe
> in beautiful things?
> I believed in beautiful
> things in Summer. Now
> all the leaves are
> gone, and it's cold."

I responded;

> "I believed in beautiful
> things when I was young,
> and naïve, Now, I'm older
> and cynical, and at peace
> with the cold & the things
> that die around Me."

> "That's very sad,"

> She said:

> "I'm at peace with that too,"

> I answered.

He was apprehensive,
trying to relish
the brevity
of being
alive,

His dangerous temperament
combined
with alcohol
was always unnerving
for Her,

like attempting to walk lightly
across broken glass
&
avoid being sliced to
ribbons,

There was a complexity
between them,

They were never marginal,
When they were together,

But there was a certain
level of anxiety,

and both knew it would
never lead to
anything

sustainable.

She walked down the aisle,
Her Father at Her side,

He stood at the altar,
waiting patiently,
    for the rest
        of His life
            to begin,

I sat in the stiff wooden pew,
    thing about how desperately
        I wanted to drink,

The priest began,
    vows were spoken,
    there was an energy
        in their gaze,

I never understood how
    two people could feel
    the way they did for
        each other,

    it just never made sense
            to Me,

So I focused on that drink,

    and My
        desperation.

I am
no good
for Them,

I will
leave before
They wake,

dressing
silently, then,
slip into the
cold morning
like a ghost,

I will disappear,

and become nothing more
than a distant memory
of something that
happened one drunken night,

They will only realize,
when They see me again,
that I was no good
for Them then,

and I'm probably
no better now.

She balanced on
        the train track
dipping Her feet
        with the grace
            of a ballerina,

"Where do You think
            they go?"

        Her voice sounded
            far away,

"I dunno, West I suppose,
        towards the Sun
            maybe..."

        I wanted to be there
            to catch Her
        when She fell,

            but She never
                        Fell.

We couldn't have
ever predicted the
outcomes we'd experience,

but there would be triumphs
that brought us to tears,
and losses that
brought us to tears,

and one way or another
it seemed to end always
in tears,

to the point where
We should've been able
to see them coming,

but didn't,

and that's what made it
all worth living for;

Not knowing what would happen,
but at the same time knowing
it would move Us,

one way or another.

I'll stay away,
I'll give You space,
I'll forget Your name,

    You wont exist,

    Something like that
       is easier said
         than done,

and now I find myself
    staring longingly
       at Her window

    hoping to catch
       just a glimpse,

    It's only been 5 days
        &
    already I can feel myself

      withering
      withering
      withering

      away,

like dead sunflowers
    on the
    window sill.

Stare at Me with
    Humid Eyes,

Make me stressed
    With Desire,

Baby, We can Fuck
    Or Make Love,

Let's twist these
    ragged sheets,

and with legs intertwined
wrapped bodies and sweat,
living forever in Sunday
        morning Sun,

We will be phantoms of
        Yesterday,

We can Fuck, or
We can make Love,

but Dear,

let's not settle for
    mediocrity.

I pulled the tiny globe
        from the mantle,
A cloud of dust rose and

                        swirled

in the light of the lamp,
It was a gift, She found,
  at some thrift store

                    for a few bucks,

Standing on the
        fire escape
I held it in my hands

                    spinning it intently,
"Your apartment is
                so dreary,"

        She said,
"I don't mind it..."
"I do. And if I'm going to be
                    staying here
that needs to change,"
"Okay,"
            I submitted.
And she placed the globe on the shelf
        with a satisfied grin,
but We are many, many
                    months removed,

The mattress has forgotten Her shape,
The birds no longer sing Her song,

and I cannot remember the sensation
        of Her touch,

I hold the tiny earth gingerly
        over the edge,

and
    let
       it
         go,
I do not need Her world
               anymore,
I am content with
      My own.

Fuck Your Love poems,
Fuck Your Love,

Give me sultry Women
in short skirts,

I want cocaine madness
& magnificent lunacy,

I want Sex & Fear &
the Police knocking
at the door,

When it's the right time
to settle,
I'll settle,

Until that time comes
I plan on burning down
Everything in sight.

Life in Reverse.

I woke,
I fell into bed fully clothed
        far past sun-up on a Sunday,
I slyly stole a pair of Her sunglasses
        and walked into the blinding light outside,
I searched the floor for boxers, shirt, jeans,
        wallet, closing the creaking door silently,
I looked upon Her in sleep & wonderment, how
        I had ended up there, Her eyes squeezed shut,

We kissed hard and long,
        tearing at each others' clothes,
        pulling each other close,
        pulling each other in,

We fumbled in pocket of laughter in the backseat
        of a cab at an unGodly hour,
        with wanting eyes & hungry lips,

We spoke drunkenly, in streams of incessant babble
        exchanging formalities,
        Her hand on my arm,
        eyes connected,
I shuffled toward Her, surgical steps, carefully
        avoiding icebergs, I inhaled deeply, preparing   for My demise
at Her hands, nervously saying
        "Hello,"   (Will this work?)
She stood on the patio, dragging on Her cigarette
        smoothly, with grace, pastel skin, lustrous,
        tawny hair, sea foam eyes,

I saw Her standing,

        Life in Reverse.

She stands in front
of the mirror again,

counting the steps
in Her head, envisioning
the motions of Her body,

when the music starts in
She is automatic, muscles
firing, teeth gritting,
        limbs flailing
                gracefully,

She falls over & over,
knees battered continually
against the hard wood floor,

bruised and sore constantly,
but She drags Herself up
off of the floor & waits
for the music to start again,

She will fall &
She will rise,

disregarding tired, aching feet,

She is relentless,
in Her pursuit of

        Perfection.

One can only
        write on the
                subject of Love

so much,

before it becomes a word
        dragged through the mud,

before it becomes perverted
        and unnatural,

before if becomes blunted,
and loses its true form,

        the word Love
        corrupts Love,

Love doesn't live in words,
            it only
            flourishes

        through Action.

We had played by the rules
We had laid out,

You keep Yours,
      and
I'll keep Mine,

and the lines were
   never crossed
        or
     blurred,

        &

We'll walk away from
     This,

exactly the same way We
    had rushed into
       It.

I should've said
You are an incomprehensible
vision of forever,
a blooming wildfire,
a gasping brook refracting
Heavenly light of
Eternity,

I should've surrounded
Myself with Your
Quddity,

You are humid air,

I am arid stygian,

We could find balance,

continuous pendulums,

I should've done
many things

that I didn't.

The Typer Shattered from the 3rd Floor

I don't listen
to the opinions
of many people,

most of their
opinions are shit,
to be honest,

Most of the time
mine is too,
to be fair,

but I've listened
to the words
of Great Men,

Who preached
Love & Compassion,
Equality & Unity,

I've seen film
of Them, marching
through the streets,
starving in beds,
for the good of
All Humanity,

Yes, most opinions
aren't worth shit,

Unless they are backed
with courageous actions.

I load the
typewriter
with a sheet
of paper even
when I have
nothing to
write.

I'll burn
holes through
the floral
border, setting
petals on fire
with My stare.

It's a force
of habit now,
get home from
working 8-hours,
load the typer,
and exhale.

Even when there's
nothing there,
just knowing the
possibility that
IT might come
at any moment,
keeps Me alive.

There I was
again,
driving away
into the
black of night,
My back to
those who
love Me so,
eyes following
the white lines
dashing in a row,
mind racing
in anxious
melancholy blue,
heart throbbing
with the sad ache
of parting with those
you hold most dear;

away, away, away,
from the certain
into the unknown.

I'm not a cynic,
and it isn't the
ugly head of
jealousy rearing,

I just never read
His shit and found
Myself wanting to
Fuck or fall in Love,

Hell, all it ever
really did was
make Me want
to drink more,

to wash the taste
of sour poetry
out of My mouth and
forget other writers
even existed at all.

Then again,
Who the fuck was I?

I read a short story
written by the
Master himself
and thought,

Well, shit. I don't
have it half as bad as
He did in His time,

I'm gonna make it,
this shitty bed,
apartment, freezing city,
I'm gonna make it,

and one day the publishers
and snot-nose editors
will see it clearly, that
I'm fucking genius,

Yeah, I'll be alright,
I'm gonna make it,

but if I have to,
I'll resort to the
9 to 5, or try My hand
at robbing banks.

So, You wanna be a writer?

Well, this is My advice;

　　On a Friday or Saturday night,
find some hole-in-the-wall
　　that You've never been to,

　　Get a good drunk on,
I suggest whiskey & beer,
　　and meet yourself someone
un-relentlessly beautiful,

　　Flirt, converse, talk
about souls & regrets,
　　fall in, and out, of Love,
without a second thought,

　　Catch a cab back to
Their place, and spend the
　　night sucking, licking,
kissing, squeezing, holding,

　　and the next day lay it
all out on the page, and if
　　You go home alone instead,
write about that.

　　Experience first,
then sit Your ass in the chair
　　and Write!

I have
real world problems,

rent, car payments,
insurance, medical care,
job security, real, true
unromantic loneliness,
bad heath, poor diet,
alcoholism, nicotine addiction,
and the list goes on...

Writing used to be
My only escape,
it was all I had
that was pure.

Now, it's work, it's
4 or 5 hours behind
the typer a night,
and countless hangovers
in the early morning,

but I've a taste now,

of what it can be like
to allow strange people
to witness the beauty of
tearing Myself apart
on the page,

the feeling consumes Me.

Cliff told Me that if this was what I really wanted, this whole writing
thing, that it
would take the patience of a Monk,

"D," He started in His Southern twang,
"You're gonna hafta really be at it Kid,
whether You think it's there or not,
Ya gotta put those damn words on the page,

over & over & over,

and if Ya got 'IT' then the diamonds will show,

keep swingin' that pick."

Good ol' Uncle Cliff, Ti-Jean's pool partner,
master of the "Jesus Christ" shot down in
sandy St. Pete, normal at the famed Wild Boar,

Well, Cliff,

Here I am behind this silly machine, night
after night, trying to knock'em out,
swinging away like a prizefighter, like
a miner with a furious and dedicated nature

Swingin' that pick,
mining for diamonds.

So I loved
Bukowski,

So He's been
an influence,

That's how this
game works,

It's called tradition
for a reason,

Buk's influenced Me
like Fante did Him,

We discover writers
who speak to Us

and then borrow
bits of style

until We are confident
enough in ourselves to
develop Our own.

The dog lies His
      head in My lap,

I am trying to work,

I am trying to create genius,

      and all He craves is Love,

I scratch behind His ear
         and coo,

"Soon, My friend,
    soon We will sleep,"

Somewhere behind His eyes
      He knows,

"Soon, My friend,"

    I tell Him,

"Soon We will curl up
      together,
    Safe and Undisturbed,
     together,
 & We will lay like that,
   waiting for the Sun
     to peak over the
  roofs far in the distance,
 making everything new
              again,
Until then, let Me fight against
    the fray,
let Me try to touch genius."

Who in their
right mind
would want
to be a writer?

it's such a
self-destructive
path to follow,

torturing Yourself
over something that
seems so trivial
in the wakes of reality,

My only advice
to potential
writers or poets
is this;

Don't do it,
but if You feel
that You must,
strap in and
prepare Yourself
for one long and
bumpy fucking road.

People sometimes
ask Me if what I write
is based on truth
or shit that's
really happened,

I tell Them,
"Parts of it,"

and when They ask,
"What parts?"

I answer,
"Whatever parts
You choose to
believe in."

If You're going to
be a critic, then
damn it, be a critic,

But if You plan on
being a writer then
put the blinders on
and just fucking write;

There's a story about
when Bukowski could've
met Burroughs, and Burroughs
could've met Bukowski,

(You can read about it
in one of their books,
I've forgotten which)

But neither really cared
to because They were too
worried about saving
their own asses,

and in the end, They
never met and neither
was any worse for wear,

Do what You know You
need to do to and
let sleeping dogs lie.

The typer stares
at Me from across
   the room while
   I'm laying on
the couch trying
   to relax for once
   in My miserable life,

   I tell Myself, "No,"
   that I won't fall
   for the trick,
   that I need to
   stay away from it,
   and keep the small
   bits of Myself
   I have left,

   But it stares
   like a woman scorned,
   mocking Me,

   "Get over here,
    you lousy prick,
    touch Me, abuse Me,
    I'm all You've
    got left."

   And I hate when
   I'm wrong, and
   it's right, and
   here I am again,

   throwing dirt
   on My own grave.

I hate being
a writer,

I wish I
could quit
this racket,

I should have
been a banker,
or pumped gas,

Writing is
terrifying
and depressing
and lonely,

but I'm no good
with numbers,

and I'm too
stupid to
pump gas.

How to correctly and
advantageously stand on
            the shoulders of
                    Giants;

    Read;
    Miller
    Hemingway
    Dostoyevsky
    Bukowski
    Kerouac
    Ginsberg
    Burroughs
    Thompson
    Faulkner
    Fante,

    Ect.

Find where They fell flat,
where You found yourself
yawning, or distracted by
        the cat toying with a moth
            flying desperately around
                the lamp – Figure out the
                    hole in their game and

            avoid the same traps.

            Be different by studying
            those who were different

                    before You.

The words leap out
of My forehead onto
the page without
thought like a strange
form of telepathy,

I don't feel My fingers
hit the keys, They
move mechanically,
like a seasoned
pianist in harmony
with his instrument.

churning out beautiful music,

never hearing the product,
so intensely focused He is,

Only the crowd erupting
in applause,
when it is
finally over.

I'll never make
        My living
        off this.

These words won't
        ever truly
        nourish Me,

I live in the 9 - 5
        World,

putting in hard, long
        8 hour perspirations,

        day after day
Monday to Friday,

        trying to replenish
        the pieces over
        the weekend,

I still never really feel
                Whole
come Monday morning,

        I'll live and die
        by the alarm clock,

Just like the
        Rest of You.

I'm no good at this,
not really,
I could
even be considered
a hack, a 2nd rate
knock-off wanna-be,

But beautiful women
tell Me I write
beautiful shit, and
it feels nice,

What little Ego
I have is fed
with their baseless
and empty compliments,

So, I write, and
I feel good, and
I drink, and I
feel good, and
sooner or later
they'll catch onto
the ruse, and I'll
have to find a
new con to keep the
hunger tamed;

Maybe, I'll take up painting.

I get drunk almost
every night
off
cheap beer,

I sit down to write,
sometimes I
get out 7 or 8,
sometimes it's
only 1 or 2,

and sometimes I
jump out of bed,

rushing to the typer
        to get thoughts down,

before they vanish,

it's always there,
the poetry,

like a fridge buzzing
in the
background.

On a quest like
Don Quixote de la Mancha,

Leaving Love in the wake
of dusty forgotten roads,

Searching for courage
in the light of Tomorrow,

I was born of rain,
I will die of fire,

Everything in between
will be soft soil
        and warm air:

Take Me as I am because
        I can't stay
                long.

I never could really
produce when I had anything
        good in My life,

        I guess that's why it
                didn't work with
        the last one,

        or why I'm okay with
                Us never working,

these wounds are
                gasoline, Dear,

        There is no room
                for happiness
                        in this
                business,

There is only room
                for what there is,

        a few words,

between the margins.

Locus;

the pattern of rain
            drops in
            a puddle
            forming
            patiently.

Derision;

a man scattered
                    & scorned,
                    a tolerant
                    forlorn,

Doldrums;

swimming upon the
            forbearances
                    of a
            raging wake
                    of
                    vows,

Nescience;

the ability to
            neglect
                the
            evident
                truths,

of a

            palpitating
                        heart.

He stacked His regrets,
one atop another,
fitting together
perfectly,

like Russian nesting dolls,

      with each new contrition
He feared the tower
would topple,

But it never did,

So he piled
penance
upon
penance,

His own personal

Tower of Babel.

Pissing Over the Railing

I knew
all the
drinking
and smoking
and fucking
was slowly
killing Me,

that I was
unraveling,

but I didn't care,
I was tired
of who I was,
where I was,

the drugs,
women, and booze
were the only
chance I had
to escape these
walls I had been
building around
Myself all these years.

I piss all over
the toilet seat, I'm
drunk and stupid,
yet again.

Apparently My
coordination
is failing Me,

and I can't aim,

no bother, I'll
clean it up in the
morning.

I'll wipe the previous
days mistakes away,
per usual,

And with a clean slate
I'll make ready for
a whole new slew
of bullshit
ready to be
piled upon
My plate;

Flashbacks of Dresden:
"So It goes..."

I worshipped the bottle,
nursing hangover
after hangover,
because of it.

But the writing was good,

It came in a crashing torrent
drenching page after page.

The pile next to the typer
grew rapidly,
the crumpled dead poems
on the floor
started to dwindle
in comparison,

And the bags under My eyes,
all the headaches,
and sleep deprivation,

were merely casualties
of the civil war
raging within Me,

as I tried my damndest
to get
the word
down.

The excruciating
         Pain
that
       seared
                My
                  skin
the first time
   I was gashed
         open,

surprised Me to tears,

Now,
when I bleed,
I laugh
& revel,

at the life slowly
oozing out of Me,

satisfied with the
          knowledge,

that there is still

some
     left
          in
                Me.

I lay on My back
in the soft snow,
thick, fat flakes
falling in globs
melting against
My eyelids,

I snarled in My
best Clint Eastwood
voice and said;

"This all You got
  Up There?
  You're gonna
  try and bury Me?

  You're gonna try
  and freeze
  Me out?"

(I grinned at the lunacy
    of my current situation
    making mad Snow Angels!)

"Well lay it on Me, Big Guy.
  Paint the whole City white,

  I'll just lay here
  on My back beside
  My Angels,
  burning away."

Cigarette blues &
that cocaine drip,

The morning is
closing in on this
cold cup of Joe,

    The bags under my
eyes are indicative
        of the years gathering
        at the base of my skull,

I creak and groan
like an old house
caught in the wind,

        retreating up the
        stairs I laugh at
        the comedy that is
            growing old,

as long as I feel 25
    and drink like I'm 25
and fuck like I'm 25,

    then I'll be 25

until that last, long
            gasp of living.

His anxiety started
to boil deep in His
stomach tied in knots,

Something brushed His
leg and caused Him to
choke with dreary panic,

The wretched stench of
pressed flesh invaded
His flaring nostrils,

He felt the sickening
crawl of vomit trying
to escape His throat,

This will never end,
This will never end,

But when the doors
spread open he leapt
into the sweet air
of victorious escape;

Hell is a bus ride
    in Brooklyn.

Maybe I'll paint the windows
in a new picture,
	Maybe I'll lose My fucking mind
and hurl shit at people,
	Maybe I'll drink the world into
a blur and forgive Me,
	Maybe I'll dangle My feet off
the roof and grin,
	Maybe I'll park here and eat
the fucking ticket,
	Maybe I'm strange, have You
thought about that?
	Maybe I'll go to sleep and
have a good dream tonight,
	Maybe I'll wake up to a
living nightmare,
	Maybe I'll toss this butt
off the Fire Escape,
	And then maybe I'll toss
Myself off next,

		Make a big mess on the sidewalk,
		A great column for papers,

"Local nobody dashed to bits on the
  cold reality of failed expectation."

		Maybe I start with something
				simple,

	and go left instead of right.

Fuck it,

Throw caution to the wind,
ingest drugs, especially when
they're free,
drink until you stumble, black
out once in awhile,
have sex with random strangers
without judging yourself
in the morning,

Do it in your 20's
Do it often and without
hesitation,

Fuck regret,

Slow down when You're 30,

and when You're 50 sitting
at a dinner party don't
tell the boring stories,

Tell them about the love
affair You had with a
Mexican prostitute,
or the rude bastard You
got in a fist fight with
outside some bar you forget
the name of in Brooklyn,

Give'em the good stuff,

Let them know You
were Alive once.

We were sitting
around the fire,

I could actually
see the stars spread
across the broad
sky for once,

It was a welcome
break from the
city,

Cliff was telling a
story about His
Love Affair
with a Mexican
prostitute, that He
had in His 20's,

We drank in His words,
and every laugh rumbled
from the gut,

I sipped My beer
and stared in
marvel
at the sky,

            at it all.

I walked a few
blocks watching My
hot breath hit the
cold air and turn
into a cloud of
fog while pretending
to smoke a cigarette,

I imagined I was
hurrying to meet
some devastating
beauty at a café
and I was late,

I imagined walking
through the doors and
locking eyes,
staring at Her
over the rim of
a cup of coffee,

We would exchange
bits of clever wit,
laughing along the way,
and part in wonderful
sad ceremony back
to our separate lives;

In reality,
I was on my way to
pick up a 6-pack so
I could get drunk alone
and pass out without
a struggle.

I'm going to be
    tired tomorrow,
       again,

When it comes time
    to punch the
       clock,

& I'll have to
    answer for it
    to the higher ups,

    & I will.

I'll promise
    I will,

I'll promise
    it won't
    happen again,

but it will,

    & I'll swallow
       that pill,

    Until They fire Me,
       or,
    I change My ways,

(But I don't see that
  happening anytime
    soon.)

Bloody knuckles,
got into a brawl
with a refrigerator,

did My damndest to
duck and weave, but
I got caught,

Slow jab & a weak
hook, and now I
bleed, am bloody,

My loss is only
evident by crimson
stains on cold doors,

When inanimate objects
start winning battles
it's pretty obvious it's

time to throw in
the white towel.

We tossed all
    morals aside.

and drank,
    heavily,

We shed our skin
and splashed
in the
current,

We were only excited
to be in the
moment,

It was something
We absolutely
needed,

because We knew We
would never have
it again,

all
moments
            are

                        temporary.

I always smoke
My last cigarette
like I'm a man
about to die;

laying mortally
wounded from a
gun duel, slowly
sipping on the
cig, letting it
hang loosely
between dry lips,

I find deep
satisfaction in
each long drag,
exhaling into
the dusty wind,
I enjoy it down
to the very last
pull, then flick
it in the dirt,
close my eyes,
and sigh,
at ease,

I treat life
like My last cigarette,
like a Man about
        to Die.

I will bundle up,
    and walk
blindly through the
    cold front,

the whipping wind
and stinging rain,

I will sit on a
cracked bar stool,

        &

shake the hands of
Fitz & Jordan & Matt,

they will bring My drinks
(a shot of whiskey & beer)
without a word & a smile,

I will drink,
until I'm drunk,
then somehow
find My way home.

All of My best friends
        are Bartenders.

There were times
        when it didn't
                matter,

When I would lean against
        the bar top
                alone,

        surrounded by noise,
        tapping into Their
                frequencies,

        laughing with Them,
        unbeknownst to Them,

        and there were times
                when it did
                        matter,

surrounded by noise,
with no frequency
        of My own,

        No voice,
        nor ear to listen,

        unbeknownst to Them,

so to answer Your question
                bluntly,

        Mr. Bukowski,

I do weep,
        don't
                You?

I'm just a drunk
  who can't find My
         lighter,
I'm just a drunk,

   God damn it,

Who has lost the light,

  I saw the light,

   She walked past Me,

We locked eyes, but She

   kept on walking,

   "You'll find the light
      again,

    someday."

  I keep telling Myself,

   just keep telling

    Yourself.

Like a pious

    Catholic,
    Christian,
 Muslim,

on bended knees,
shoulder blades
jutting outward,
abdomen contracting,
gripping the edges
of the porcelain
toilet bowl, groaning
as my stomach churned
and insides emptied
out, liquid splashing
into liquid, wiping
tears from My bleeding
eyes, vowing relentlessly,

"Never again, never again
          never again..."

But I knew that was a lie,
a phrase I was using to
comfort Myself in a time
    of distress,

My mantra;

never again.

Unfortunately,
I can't afford to
    drink
                Gentleman Jack,

    I buy what's cheap and
        gets the job done,

I'd like to think some
        success will never make
                Me soft,

I'd like to believe
        the sight of blood
        won't ever make Me
                    shutter,

I've seen Them sleeping
        in the park,

 Hands out, sitting on
        the curb,

Distressed & Long gone,

I knew I never wanted to be there,
I knew given the right circumstances
                I could be,

So I dropped quarters in Their cups
                when I could,

& somewhere dark inside Me,
                I knew,

        I'd never be soft,
        & a little blood would
        never bother Me,

I toss quarters in their cups
                    &
I buy what's cheap because
        it works.

Shivering with a Cigarette, Staring into the Void

If You believe in
something, anything,
with everything
You are,

then for Christ's sake
don't ever bite
Your fucking tongue!

Speak up! Speak loudly!
make Your message heard!

Or what's the use of
speaking at all?

Stand strong by
Your convictions,

A Man without
conviction,

Is not a Man.

My checking
  account
is dismal,

yet again,

the frustration
  of making
  ends meet,

is wearing,

  from Monday
  to Friday
   I drag,

my bones,

  around the halls,
  up & down sidewalks,
  ascending stairs,
  descending stairs,

  ascending &
  descending,

continually,

  on the weekends
  I sleep like
  the dead,

immoveable, content
  with my small
       plot.

They want Us
to hate each other,

to divide is
to control, and
we blindly thrust
Ourselves in
Their traps;

No religion
encourages hate,

No person is born
with malice in
their heart,

We can choose
to be ignorant,
or We can educate
Ourselves and
learn to understand
the World through
a foreign perspective.

like the bones
were stripped of muscle
    and tendon,

exposed to the choking
grip of Winter's
    breath,

  There I stood surrounded
    by a world of
      blinding white,

nothing stirred,

everything was

  beautiful
              &
        dead.

I felt the
city breath in
deeply,

remorseless
cold air
that tightened
chests,

it grew cold.
covered in its
harsh disguise,

that would soon thaw
and reveal a
beautiful
hidden identity,

but those
cold months sitting
behind closed windows

made Me feel
warm & protected
by My walls,

and I questioned
if I ever
wanted to stray from

what I knew
was safe.

Staring
    unblinkingly
      into the vacant
                   gulf
of the raven sky,

   a single thought
    germinated
  in My mind;

No God, nor Woman
    can ever save
      Me,

Not from what I was,
or what I've become,

but I wish both the
former and latter to
    give it their
      best damn
    effort,

to prove Me wrong.

When I tried
lying to my Father
as a teenager
He would give Me
a stern look,
and in His fatherly tone
say;

"Yeah? And My ass
  sucks river water."

The thought always
made Me laugh
uncontrollably.

and He would
crack a small grin,

and We both knew
I was mowing the lawn.

for the next month straight.

I watch in
sickening amusement
        as My dog chases
            a fly
about the living
room, snapping
His strong jaws
        at it,

and part of Me
hopes he catches
and devours the
little buzzing
nuisance,

but the other
part of Me
hopes the fly
manages to escape
and survive for
another day or two,

because I know
what it's like
to run scared
from the thought
of some black
unknown trying
to swallow
You whole.

I've
grown
complacent with
My situation
and surroundings,

Something
drastic must
be done about this
at once,

Constant change
is a necessity
for a decent chance
of not dying
before you're
actually dead.

I always bet on the

L o n g s h o t,

I figured the underdog
deserves a fair shake,

Hell, I am one, after all,

I know what it's like
to have the odds stacked
against You,

But, I also understand that
when You beat those odds,
it's the sweetest victory
Your tongue will ever taste.

I was always grateful
for what They provided Me;

A semblance of normalcy,
A hand to grasp in the dark,
A place to lay My tired head,
A shot at something permanent,
Although permanence never
quite stuck,

I was grateful,

An I was never bothered when
My appreciation wasn't
met with reciprocation;

I'm just better at giving
than I am at accepting,

It's the flaw in
My design.

The filament popped,
    and I was shrouded
        in deafening obscurity,

  idiosyncratic sky,

  in the darkness
  the shower simulated
  the rain,

  I wanted to be caressed
      by white noise,

unnaturally lulled,

      scene for a
        voyeur;

      prima facie;

a Man laying in a bed,
      naked in His skin,

          verity;

a Man laying in a bed,

      at War with
            His bones,

  sleep well, obscurity.

What a cruel fate
to be born Human,

to understand
the reality of Death,

to be conscious of it,
while trying to
Live at the same time,

But do not fear Death,

closing the book
will be the easy part,

it's the living
that's going to
hurt the most.

Fall rushed in
  like a
statement,

a command,

it brought with
     it
  a creeping
    chill,

that rippled skin,
that quivered bones,

    an afflictive
        fret,

signaling the
   beginning
       of the
          end,

  of another
    beginning.

My head hung,
face against palms,
lips mouthing the
prayers of My
Father, eyes
tightly shut,
deathly afraid
of the magnitude
of unimaginable
sooth, I made
supplications
under a blood
red moon, I
implored the
oil sky, for
herald, seeking
sanctification
through penance,

eyes shut tight
mouthing the
prayers of My
Father,

under the
blood red
Moon,

The rain dances
furiously against
   the slick black
      asphalt,

I am sitting
in My great grandmother's
   old recliner
staring out the window,

     watching,

the dog is curled up
   on the sofa,

I am sitting in a
   dead woman's chair,

We
  are
     just
        here.

The windows rattle
in My apartment,

They shudder angrily
against the howling wind,

but, I am no longer afraid
of shuddering panes,
or creaking homes,

I don't believe in
fairy tales, or magic,

I don't believe in the
monsters that reside
underneath the bed, anymore,

Every monster or ghoul
I have met,

walks casually through the
daylight, hidden by the
disguise of normalcy:

Monsters exist,
Ghouls are real,

But We can only see Them
if We are willing to
suspend disbelief.

I listen to the radiator
hiss & feel the warmth starting
to emanate from the large
iron ribs, through the
window the wind is a hushed
swoosh blowing through the
last remaining leaves that
cling desperately like the
    last bits of skin to
        a skeleton;

  I think of Spring
  I think of nothing,
  I think of crawling into
  My warm bed,

  and going to sleep.

On the I-90
doing 75 on
My way back
to Buffalo,
surrounded
by black,
following
the lines
going down the
center of the
road,

A wave of
nausea wracks
My body and
I groan,
Almost home,
Almost safe,

So I keep
driving straight
into the
distance,
where the night
swallows the
road,

and beyond.

I miss My Father
       My Mother,

being able to
     embrace them
        both,

     the way their arms
         envelope Me,

     making Me feel safe,
             protected,

     like a child, again,

        but I can never
           go back,

        none of Us can
           ever
                go
                   back.

Icarus was a
damn fool,

jealous of the
freedom of birds,

because of this
He chose unwisely,

rather to fly into
the burning sky,

than glide into the
cool spray of the ocean,

He lost His sense of
Humanity with those wings,

The simple Man knows;

it's better to dive into
the unknown depths of tomorrow,

than to

Fly head first proudly
into flames of destruction,

Learn how to swim.

From a rooftop
        in Brooklyn,

The J-train rumbled by
     as the misery of
another day ending
          glinted off
          its silver fluid,

   I squinted at the World,

   My brother handed Me
              a cold beer,
   as We sat together
              in silence,

waiting,

for the night to
     swallow existence.

I
toss a
quarter
into their
cup,

Eyes
on the
ground and
keep it
moving,

I have
My
diseases
to deal with
too.

We as Human Beings
are capable of such fucking
    extraordinary accomplishments;

We explore the goddamn galaxies,
We build magnificent structures,
We learn to cure diseases,
We scale impossible mountains,
We explore the deepest oceans,
We traverse countries,
We create beautiful pieces of art,
We wage Wars against wrong doings,
We triumph against the greatest
odds and stand strong in the
wake of inexplicable tragedy,

And still, We walk through the
streets looking at each other
with distrust and hate
in Our eyes,

Because of the color of skin,
Because of the God We believe in,
because of political identity,

We are able to perform feats
that seem otherworldly on an
almost daily basis,

But We are still unable to
Love each other as People,

How is that possible?

My room is a mess,
My car is a mess,
My life is a mess,

But there is something
beautiful hiding within
the disarray of everything,

The scattered paper on the
floor, beer cans on the
mantle, empty cigarette packs
on the coffee table, dirty
dishes in the sink,

There is something beautiful
hiding in it,

I will find it.

I will show the world
how attractive ugliness
        can be,

I will expose it for
You all to see it

how I do.

Standing barefoot
on the cold iron grate,

30 feet above the
cold cement,

Lifeless,

from up here I
see sedated rooftops,

severe chimneys,

vacant window,

apparitions
of
Our past,

From up here
I see

Nothing,

nothing
at
all.

I'm not a Religious Man,
but there are nights where I
unfold on the piles of leaves
that gather in small drifts against
the base of the trees in the quiet
park on tinted Autumn night;

Leaning in nervous leisure,
tugging deftly on a cigarette,
eyes cast upwards through the
web of shivering branches
toward the omniscient
foreverness of Midnight,

I pray, in a grave hush;

"Dear God, Allah, Buddha,
whoever hears My soft cries;

        I know I am an insignificant speck,
        caught in the magnitude of an
        infinite cloud of cosmic debris,
        but I am here, still, and I was
        promised peace, Heaven, enlightenment,
        and I have received none;
            but I am here, still;
        all I ask is a sign, a vision, an
        awakening, show Me something!"

and I wait in silence,
watching the dead leave scatter
in the breeze, pulling on
a cigarette, to no avail,

There is My answer; the Silence
                        of Gods.

An abstract thought;

Go on a pilgrimage to Lowell
                    to Los Angeles
                    to Mexico
                    to Bunker Hill,

        Fugazzi's, The Vesuvio, The Wild Boar,

        Go to St. Pete where Clifford sprang forth:

San Francisco is a holy place,

        There are spirits dwelling
            in Berkley shacks,

        Deliver mail, develop calluses,
            become a brakeman on the
                railways,

        For Christ's sake,

        A carpenter with no calluses
            is no carpenter at all.

        Hozomeen is calling!
        Hozomeen, Hozomeen!
        You gorgeous ridge of
            Desolation,

        Do not be a Hemingway & check out early,
        Do not be a Salinger & hide Yourself away,

Be one of those sad geniuses that
rebelled against the promise of

                certain mortality.

Make amends,
Make amends,
Make amends,

Lay Yourself
at the feet
of those You
have wronged,

beg, grovel,
be steadfast
in Your pursuit
of forgiveness,

make Your universe
        right,

expect rejection &
        hardship,

but be constant
in Your quests,

a galaxy left
uncorrected

will certainly
        implode.

I sit on the
sill of the open
     window,

for hours at a time,

watching people,

walking through the parking
     lot, past the gas pumps,
     disappearing into the store,

They emerge with plastic bags
     carrying things,
  (It doesn't matter what.)

     Then they disappear again,

past the branches out of sight,
down dark and narrow roads,
into cars and drive off,

never to be seen again,

     I've grown comfortable
     in their routines,

     growing numb on the
       window sill,

     watching the People.

The moon is beautiful tonight;
it hides behind
black clouds, then suddenly
it's there.

Do You remember the night
We were walking back from
the bar, and We stopped to
look at it, like a giant
dripping blood-red flame?

And it was so big, sitting
between those buildings,
like We could reach out &
cradle it in Our hands?

That was a good night.

No more Love poems;

You want to listen
   to the melody?

Then stand on the edge
   of a body of deep
         water
while the waves endlessly
         lap,

You want forever?

lay on Your back and
observe the endless
         Universe,

You want to pledge
   allegiance to something
You can't touch?

         join a cult;

Don't let the shiny
   packaging spin
            You;

There's a reason the
saying goes:

         "Believe nothing that You hear,
            and only half of what You see,"

If you can't reach out and touch it,
            it's not part of your
                  reality.

Crushed by the weight
of an
allegory,

brain wracked
by the
consequences
of tomorrow,

standing in the
eye
of the
storm

can be calming,

if You're
at peace

with the
inevitable.

allow Yourself
to be
at
Peace.

I say goodnight
to the fluorescent
lights illuminating
the night,

Goodnight Clouds, Moon, City,
strange inhabitants,

Goodnight, Girl I Love,
Goodnight, body next to Her,

Goodnight Dog,
Goodnight Ma,
Goodnight Pa,

Goodnight Brooklyn,
Goodnight Buffalo,
Goodnight New York,
Goodnight Rochester,
Goodnight Kansas,
Goodnight California,
Goodnight Texas,

Goodnight! Goodnight!
and Godspeed into
Your journey
into tomorrow!

Goodnight,

and wish Me luck.

The dog's head hangs
out of the window
through the screen
torn to ribbons,

like some kind
of gargoyle,

We're fine with
being shut-ins,
sometimes We linger
out on the fire escape

watching life cinema,

; Scenes from the Fire Escape ;

Underwater Mountains Publishing.
Elias Joseph Mennealy & Ryan Christopher Lutfalah.
A Private Company.